The DRawbRidge ©

Random Things: Volume 1

All Artwork by: Paul Gill.

Published by The Drawbridge.
www.enterthedrawbridge.com
www.paulgill.com

ISBN 978-1515103080

For my family, friends and supporters,
and of course, my Little B.

This book contains a collection of random sketches and doodles (in no particular order) from the past year. Some are funny, some are weird and some have chickens in them. In all honesty, I never know what's going to show up on that piece of paper when my pen hits it...and I hope they're as entertaining for you as they are for me.

Enjoy them for what they're worth...
at least five bucks...at least.

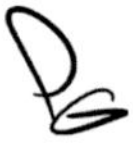

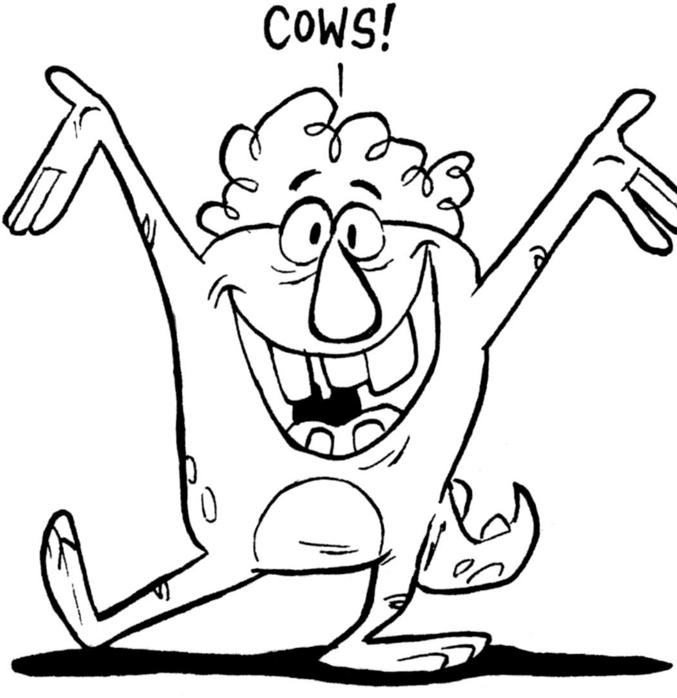
COWS!

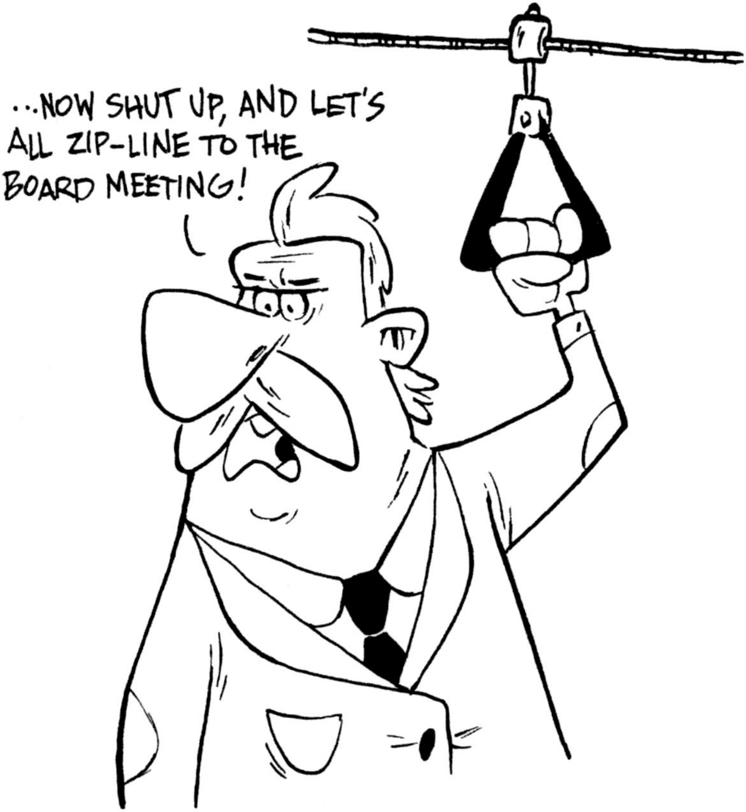
...NOW SHUT UP, AND LET'S ALL ZIP-LINE TO THE BOARD MEETING!

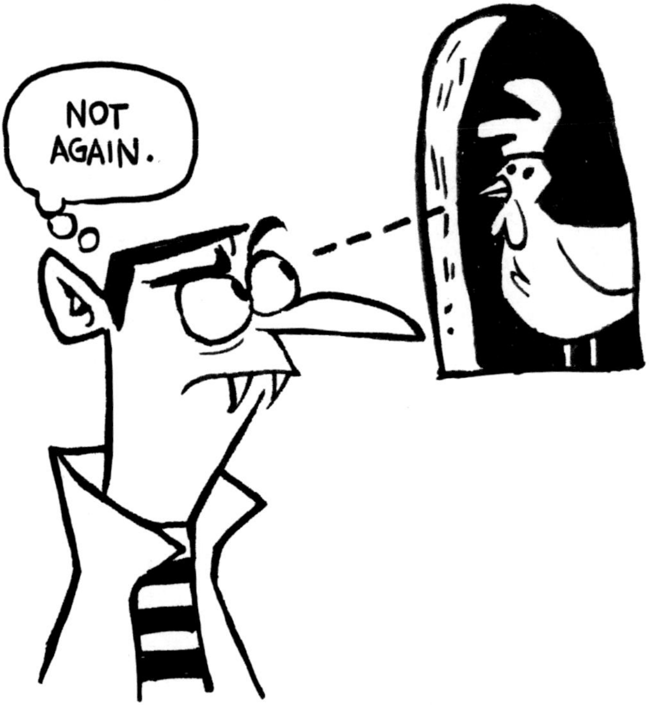
NOT
AGAIN.

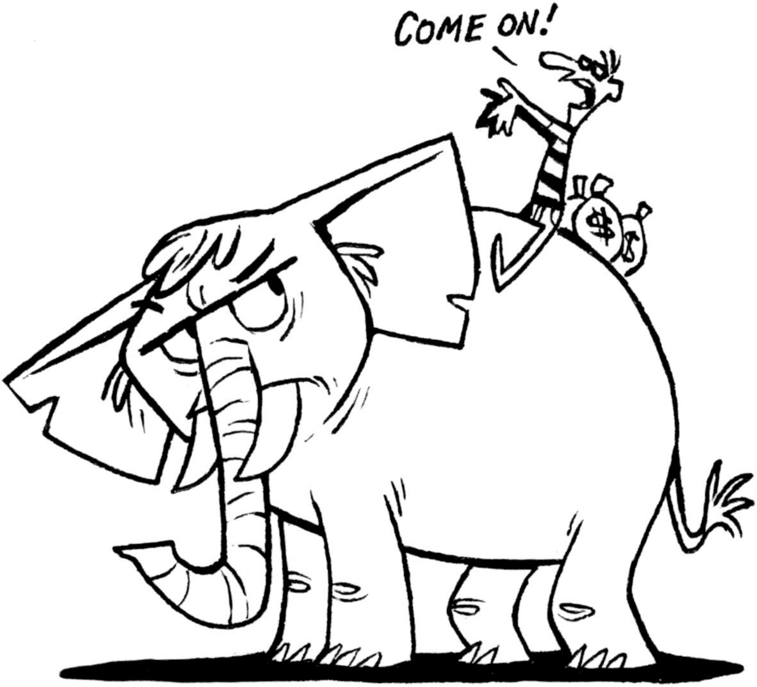
COME ON!

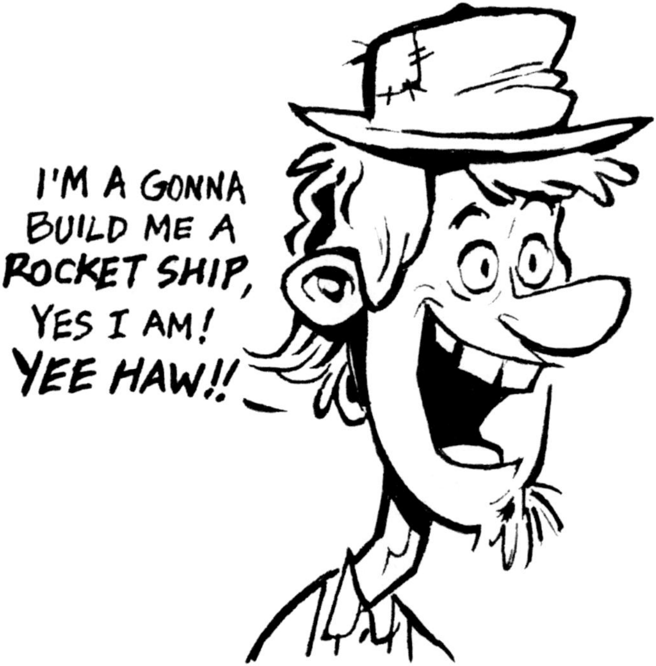
I'M A GONNA
BUILD ME A
ROCKET SHIP,
YES I AM!
YEE HAW!!

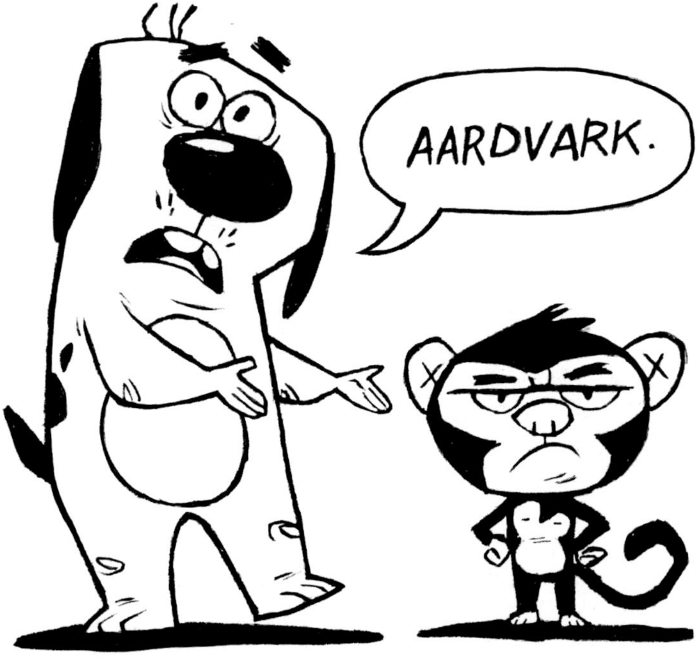
AARDVARK.

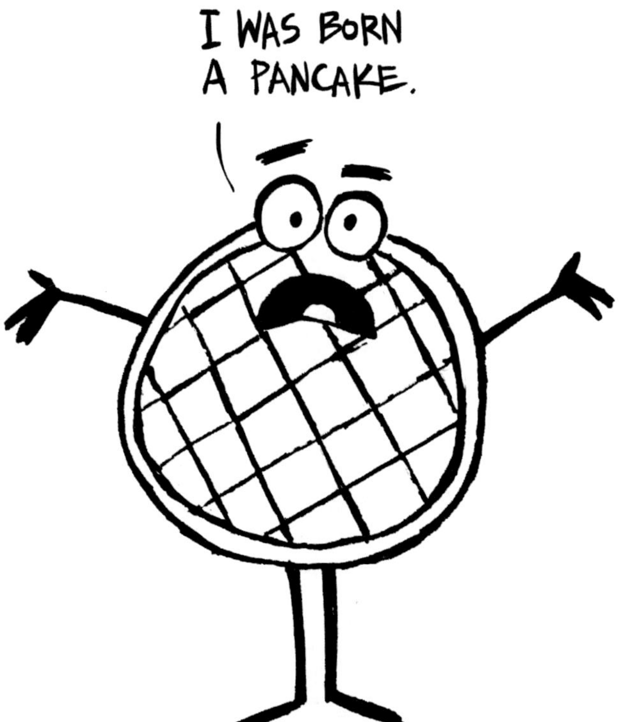
I WAS BORN
A PANCAKE.

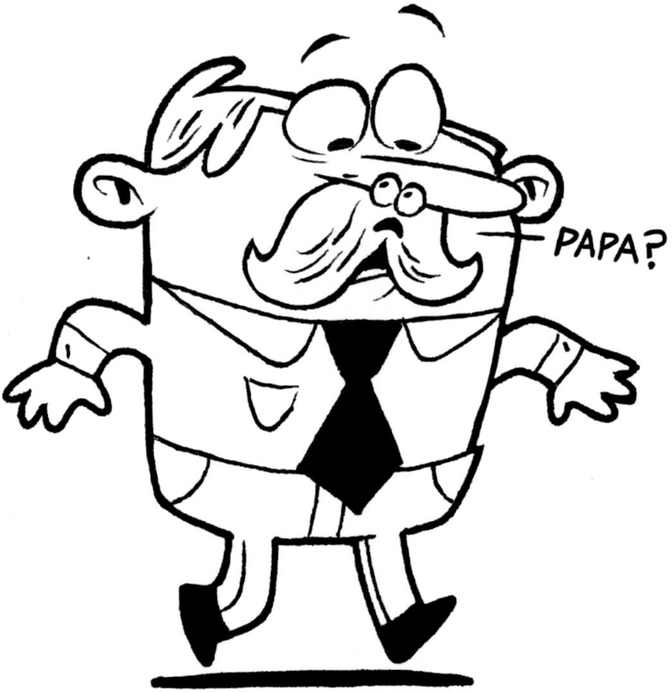
PAPA?

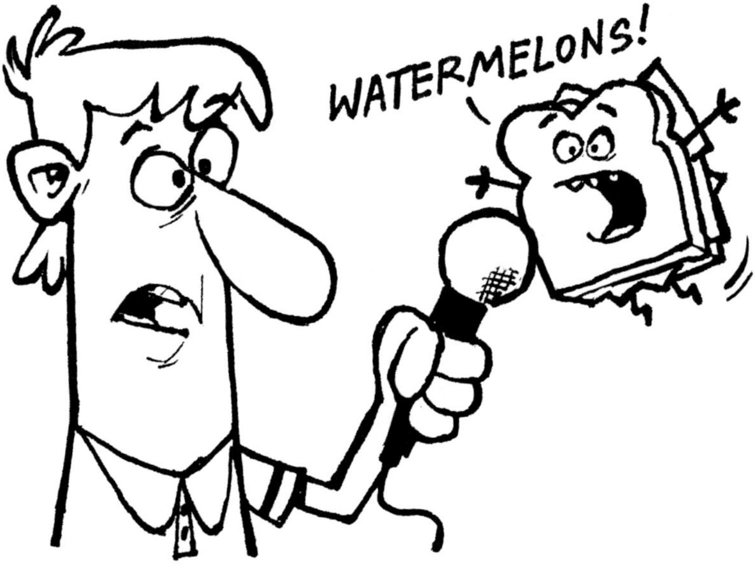
WATERMELONS!

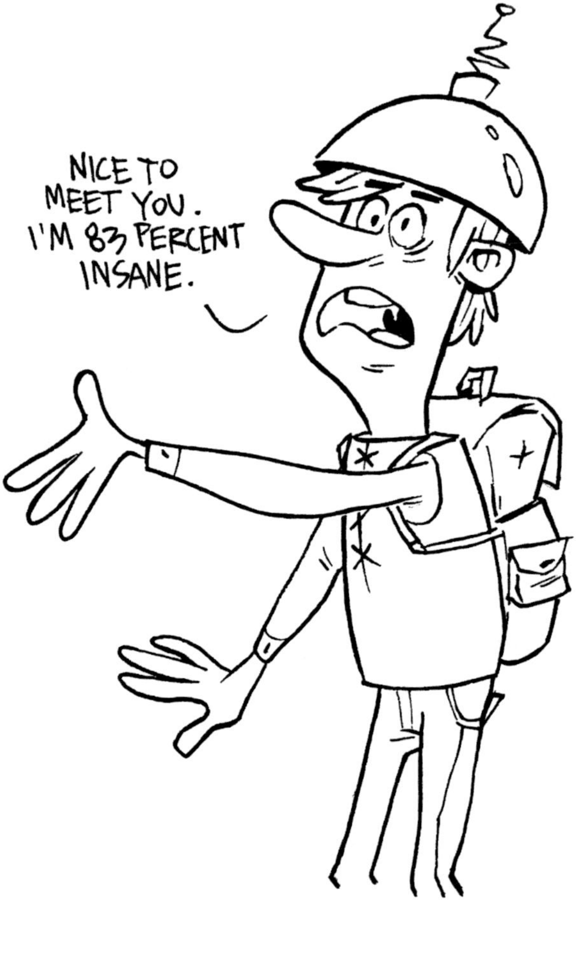
NICE TO MEET YOU. I'M 83 PERCENT INSANE.

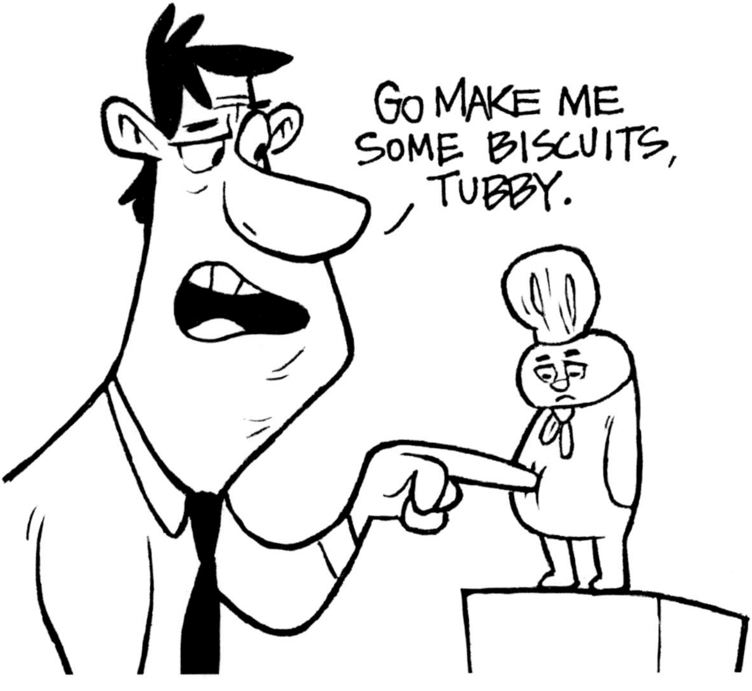
GO MAKE ME SOME BISCUITS, TUBBY.

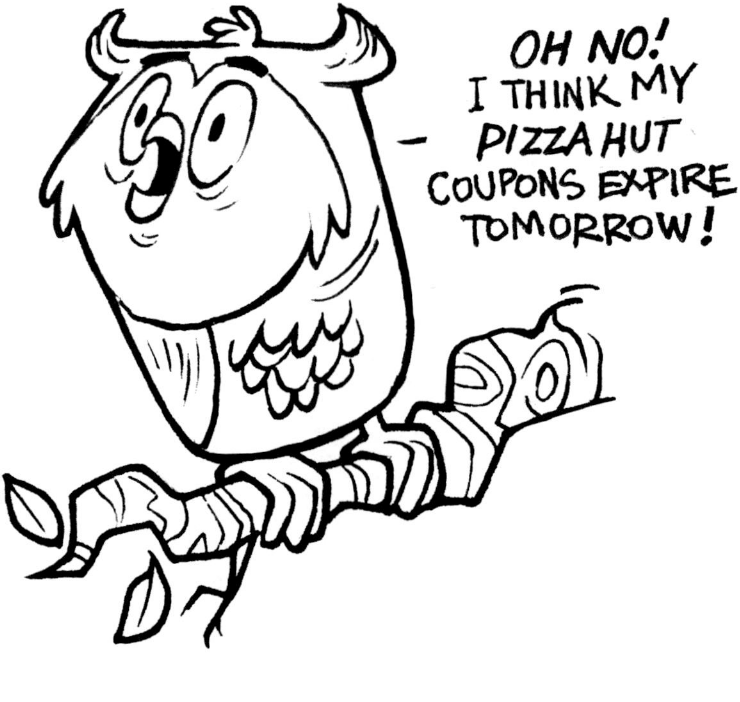
OH NO!
I THINK MY
PIZZA HUT
COUPONS EXPIRE
TOMORROW!

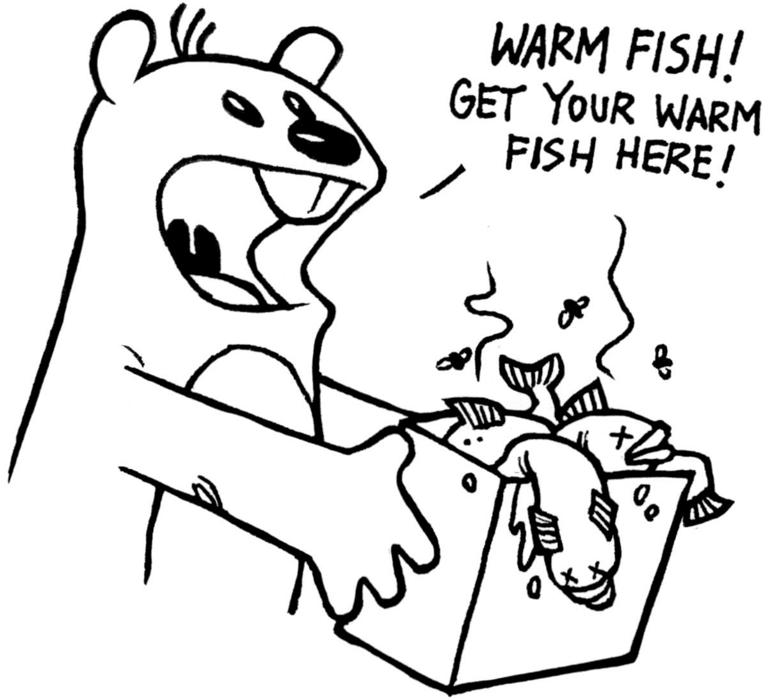
WARM FISH!
GET YOUR WARM
FISH HERE!

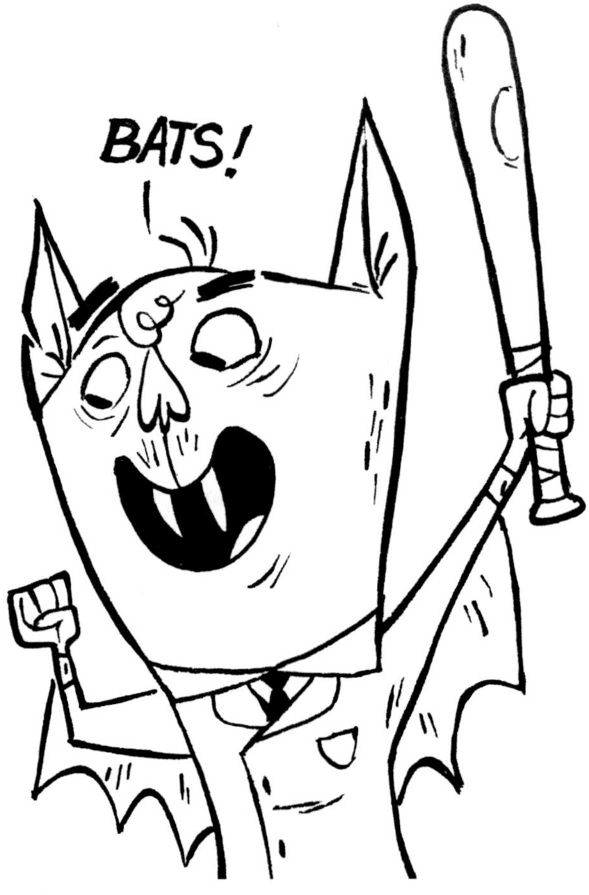
BATS!

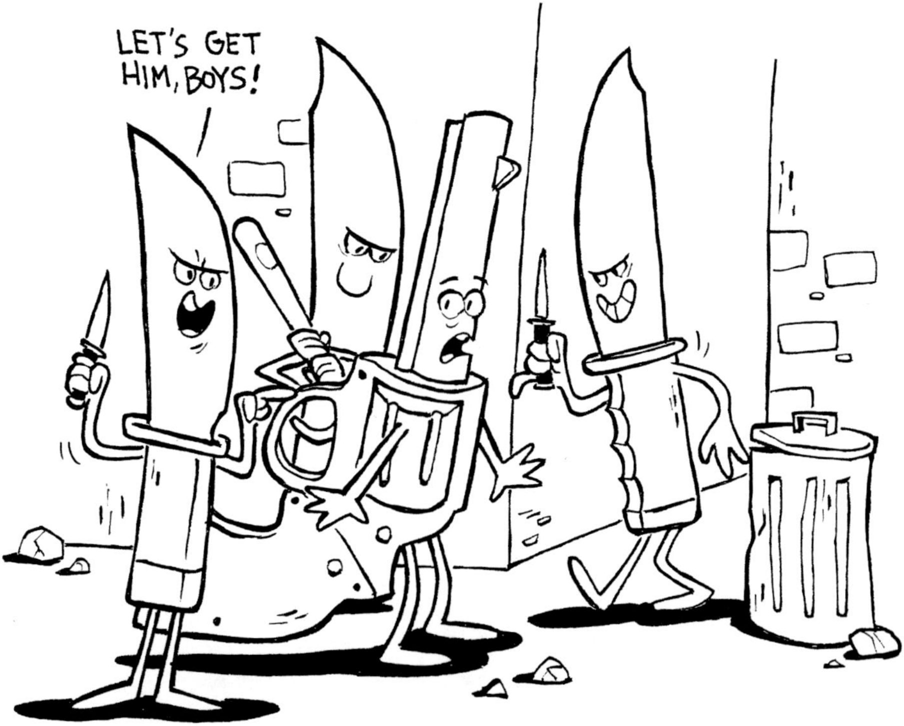
LET'S GET HIM, BOYS!

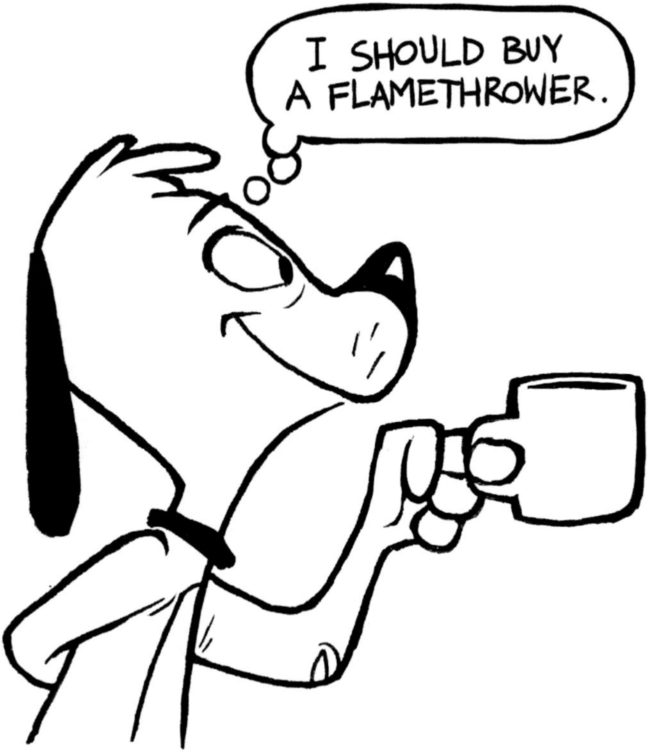
I SHOULD BUY A FLAMETHROWER.

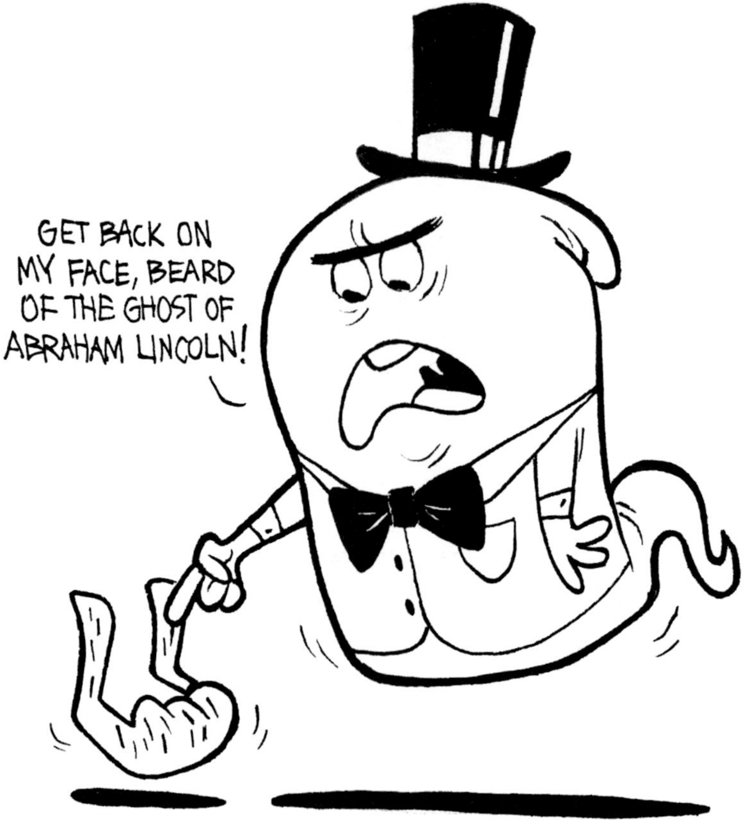
GET BACK ON MY FACE, BEARD OF THE GHOST OF ABRAHAM LINCOLN!

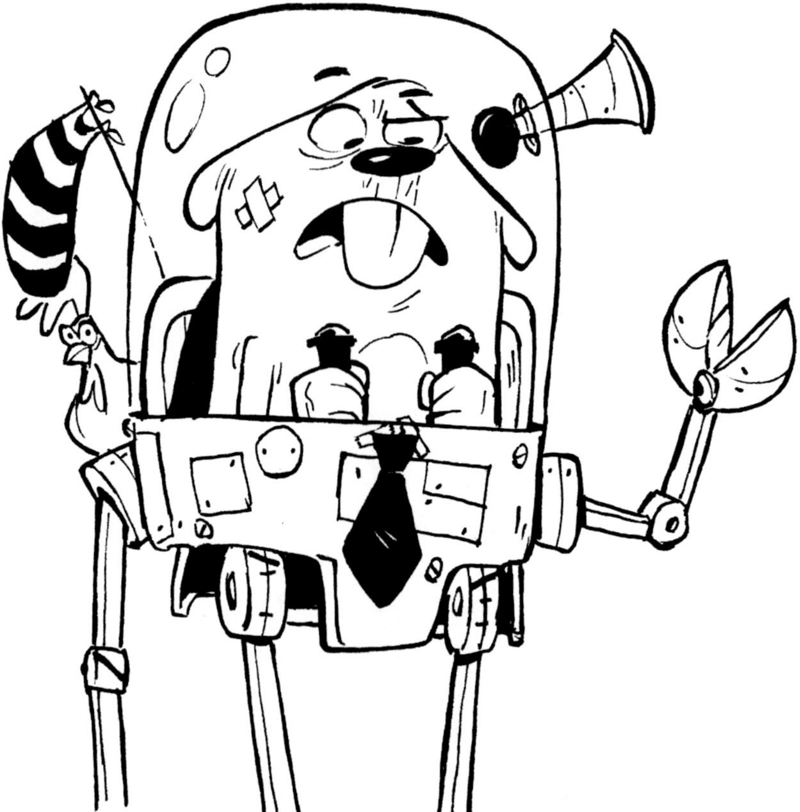

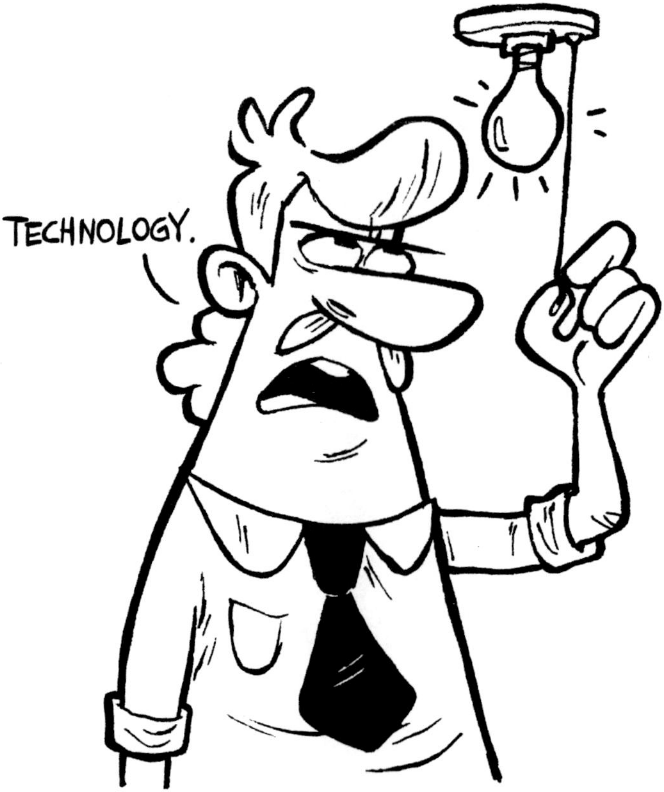
TECHNOLOGY.

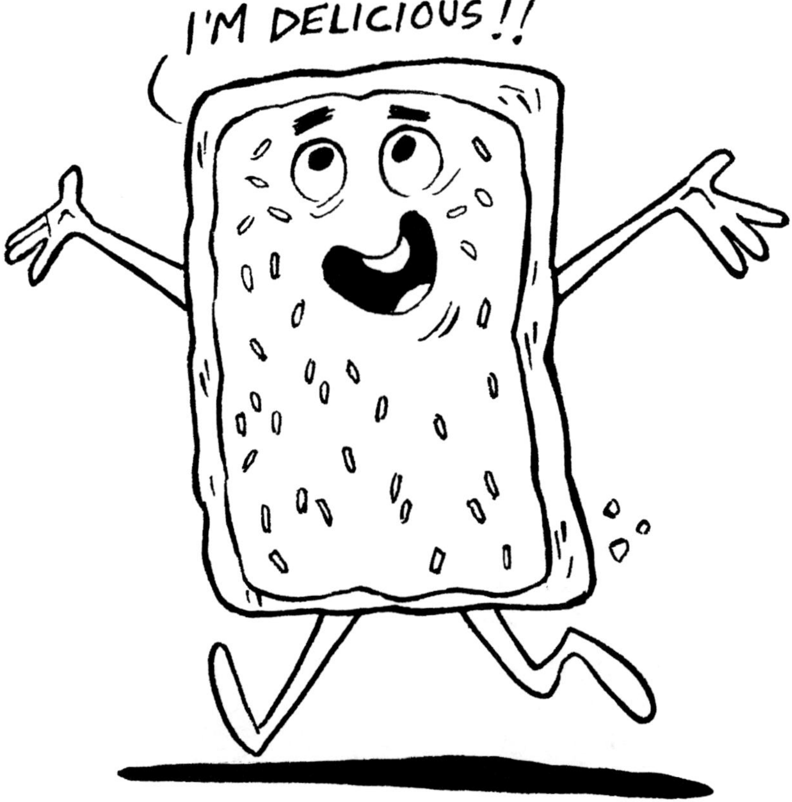
I'M DELICIOUS!!

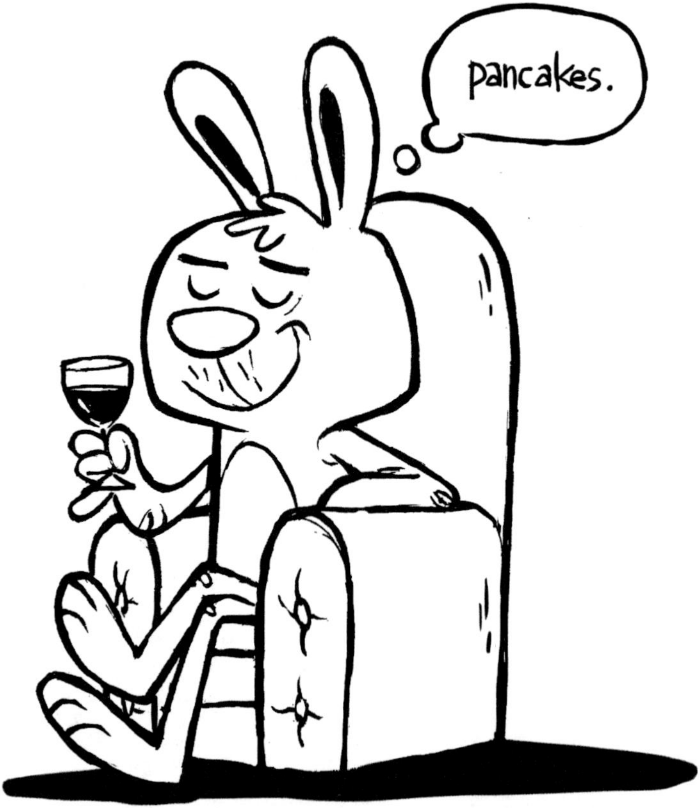
pancakes.

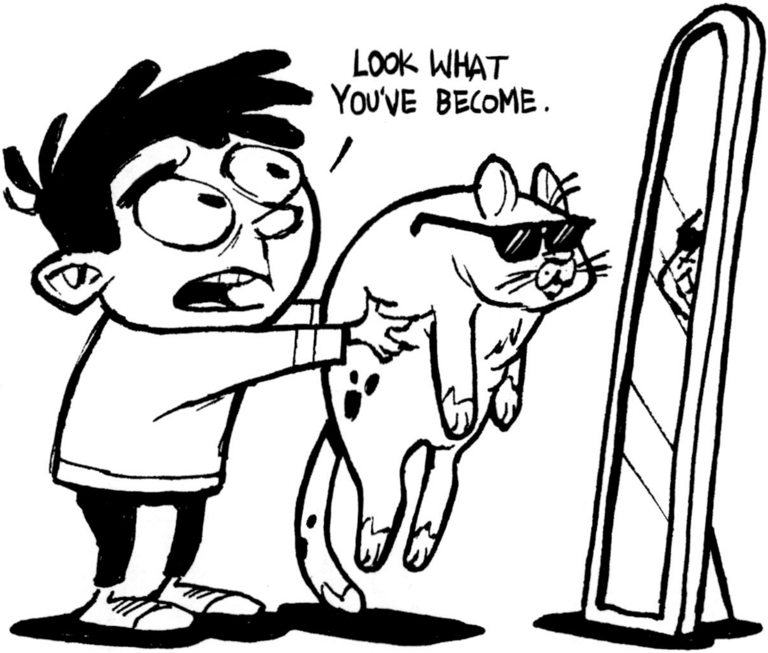
LOOK WHAT YOU'VE BECOME.

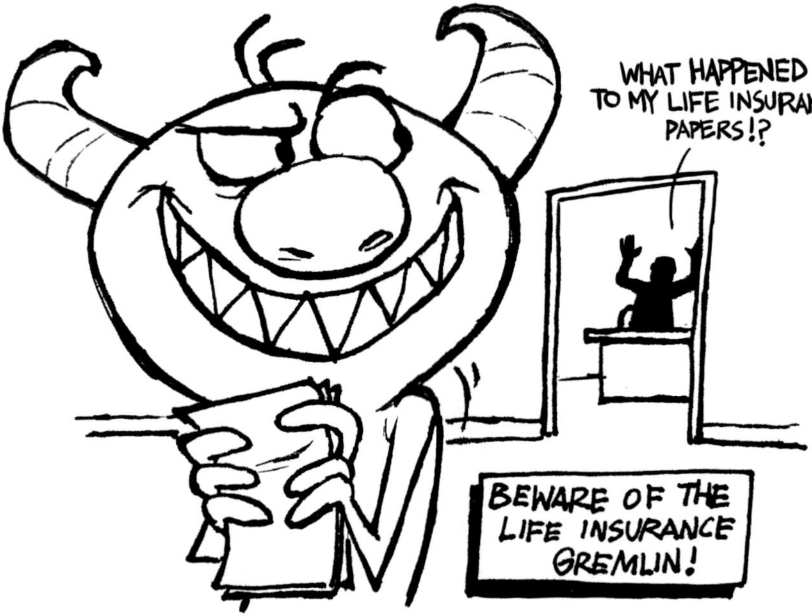
WHAT HAPPENED TO MY LIFE INSURANCE PAPERS!?
BEWARE OF THE LIFE INSURANCE GREMLIN!

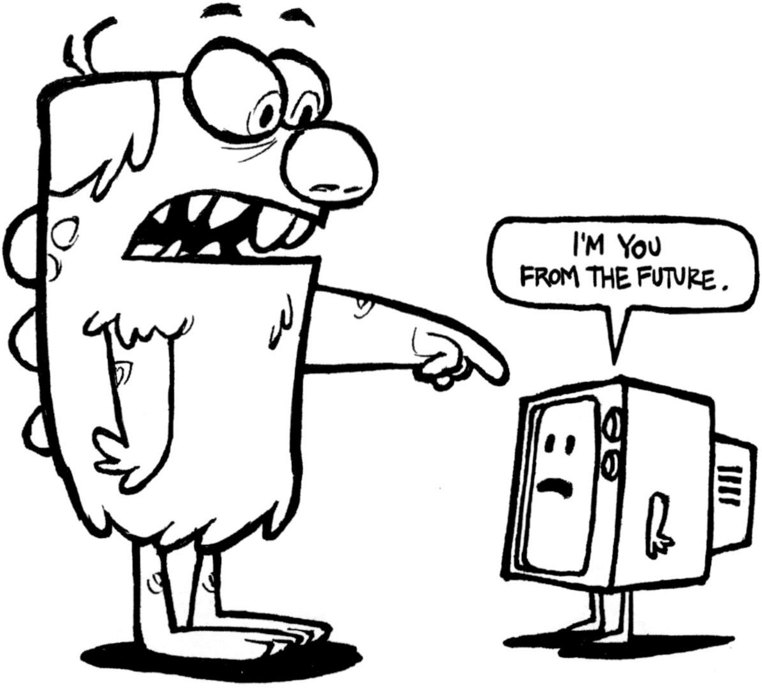
I'M YOU FROM THE FUTURE.

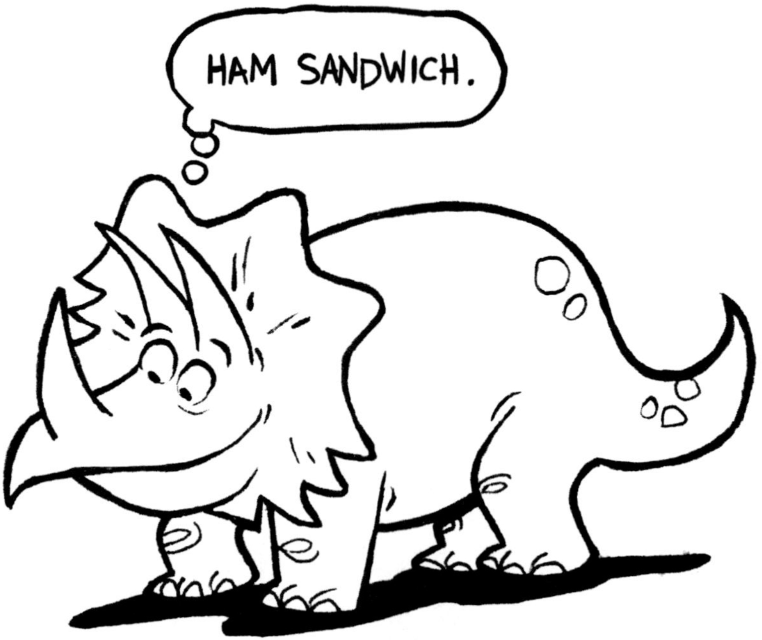
HAM SANDWICH.

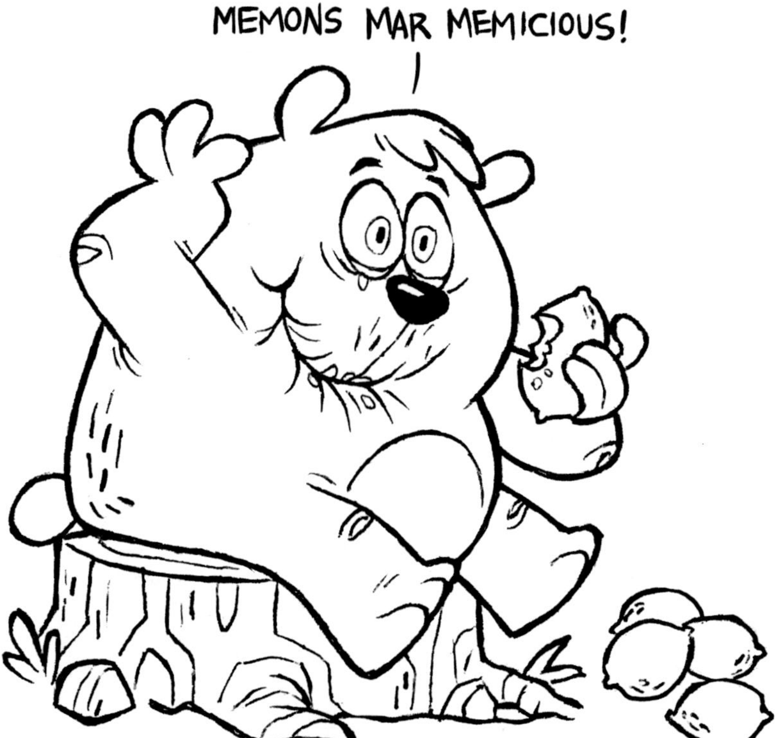
MEMONS MAR MEMICIOUS!

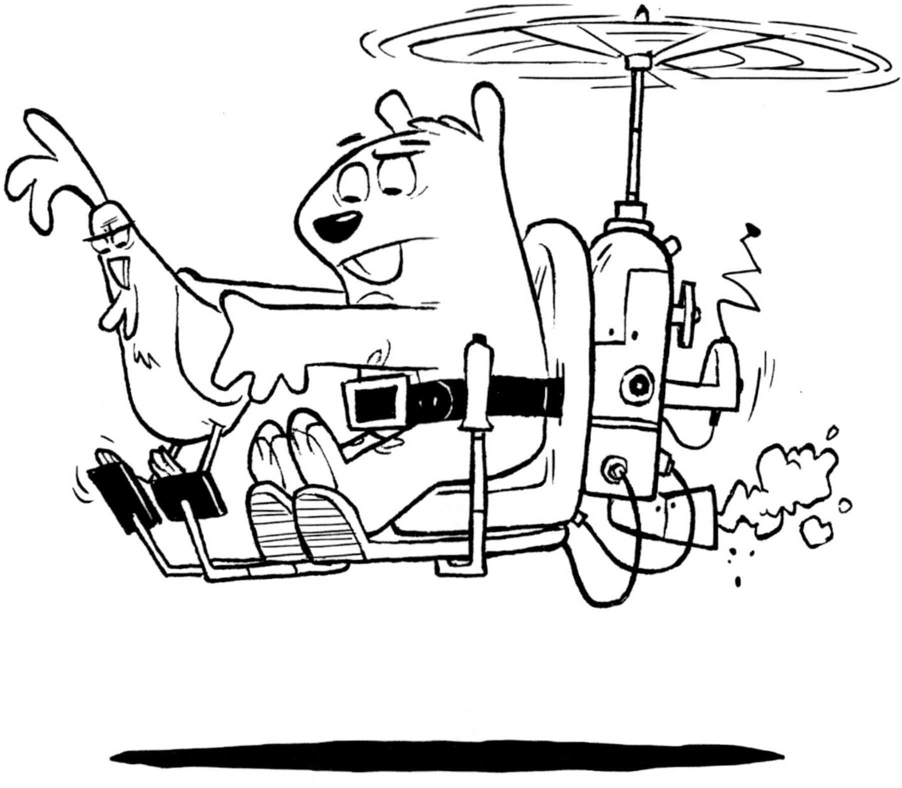

IT WAS FRANKLIN'S LAST
DAY AS A MARSHMALLOW...
TOMORROW HE WOULD BECOME
PART OF SOMETHING BIGGER...
A RICE KRISPY SQUARE.

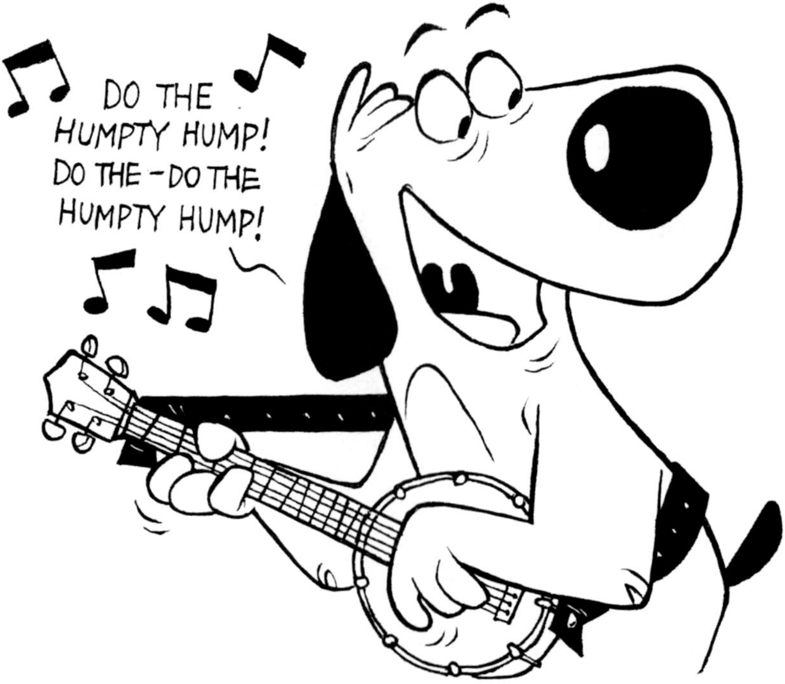
DO THE HUMPTY HUMP! DO THE–DO THE HUMPTY HUMP!

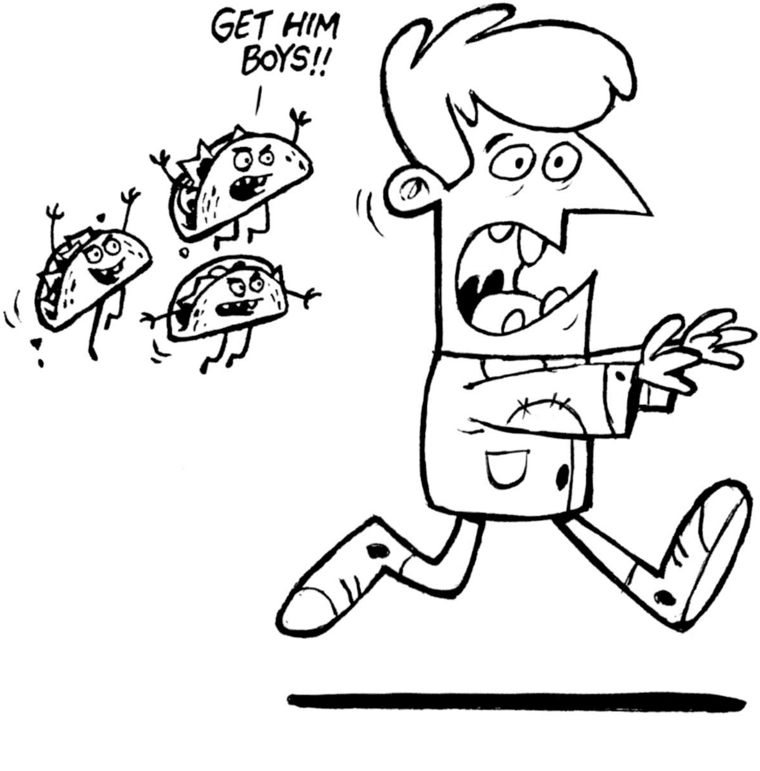
GET HIM BOYS!!

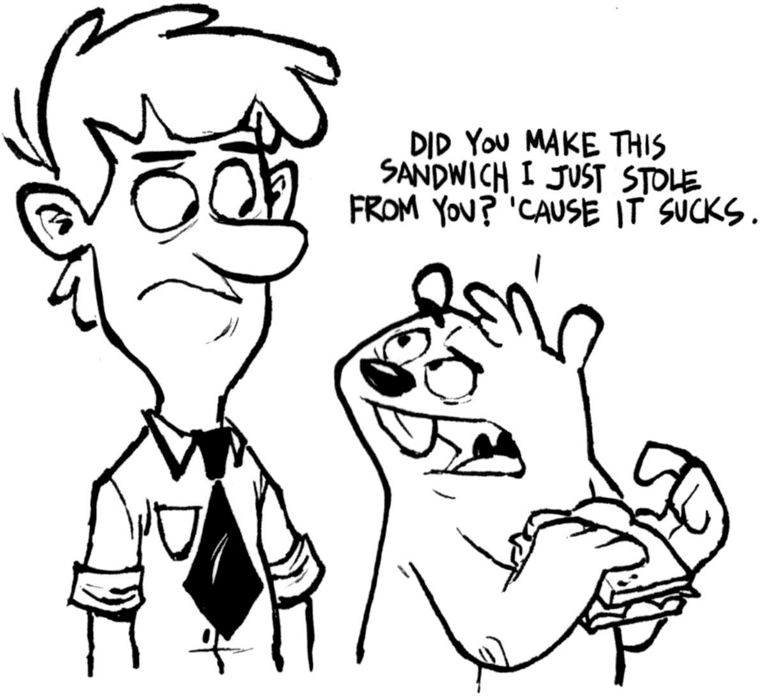
DID YOU MAKE THIS SANDWICH I JUST STOLE FROM YOU? 'CAUSE IT SUCKS.

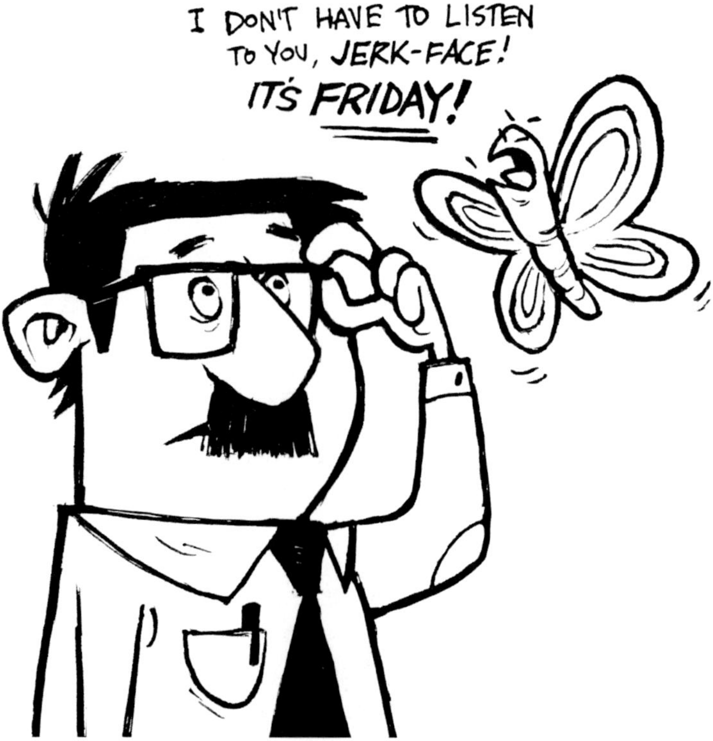
I DON'T HAVE TO LISTEN TO YOU, JERK-FACE! IT'S FRIDAY!

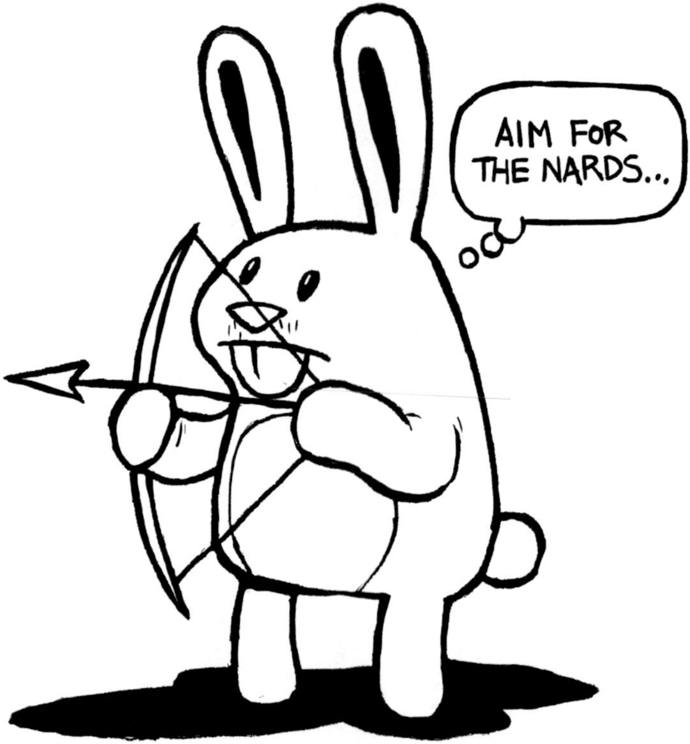
AIM FOR
THE NARDS...

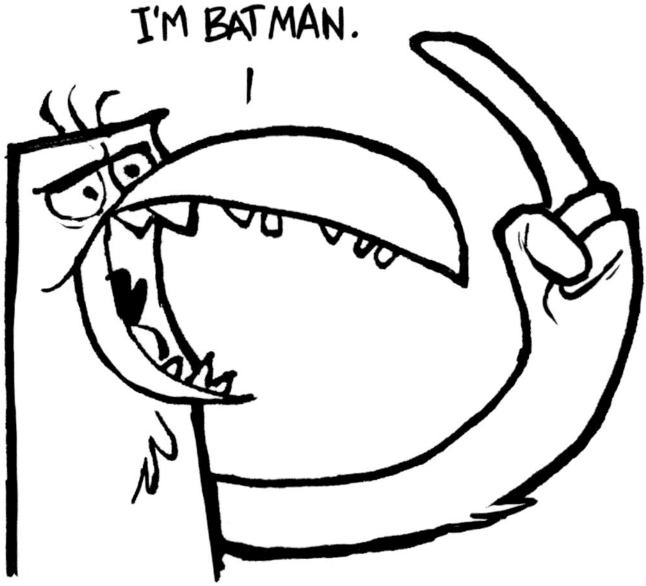
I'M BATMAN.

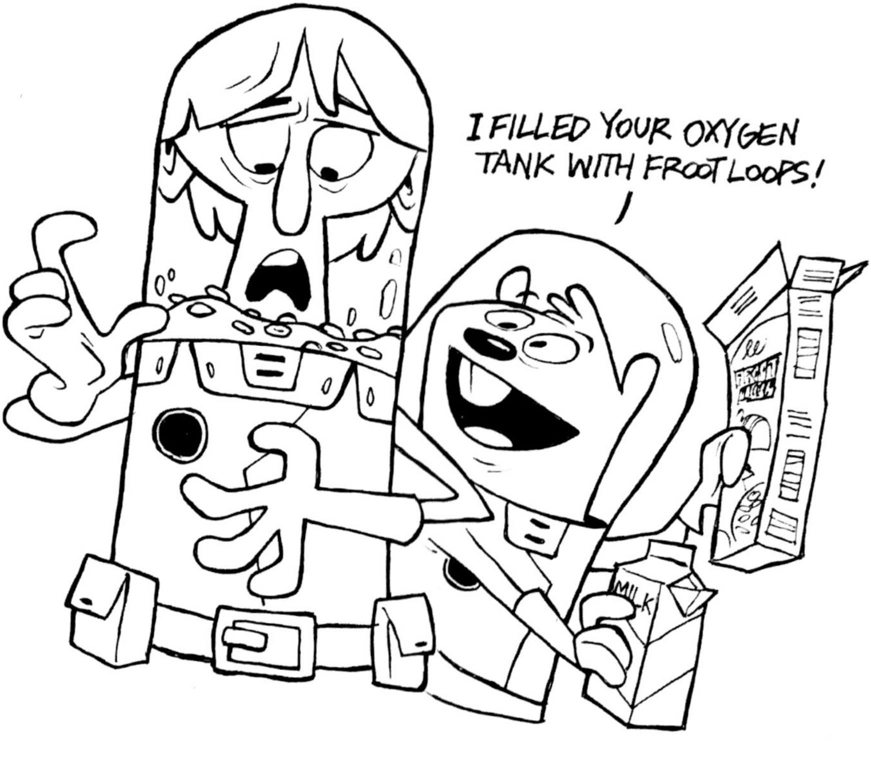
I FILLED YOUR OXYGEN TANK WITH FROOT LOOPS!
MILK

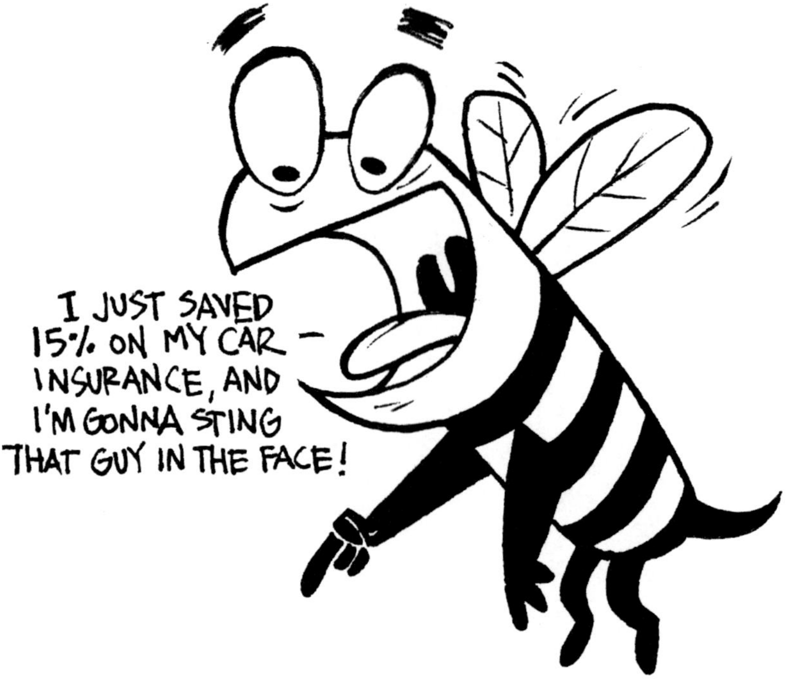
I JUST SAVED 15% ON MY CAR-INSURANCE, AND I'M GONNA STING THAT GUY IN THE FACE!

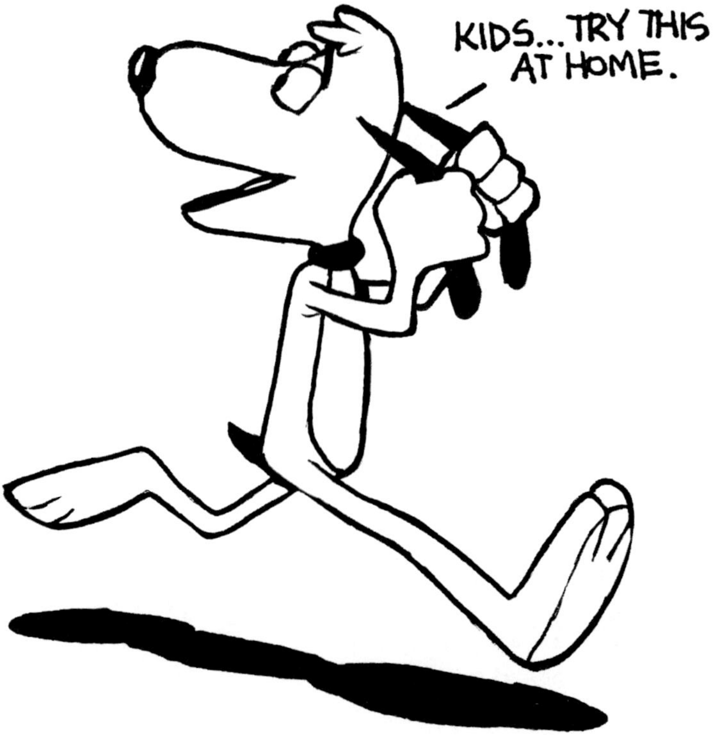
KIDS... TRY THIS AT HOME.

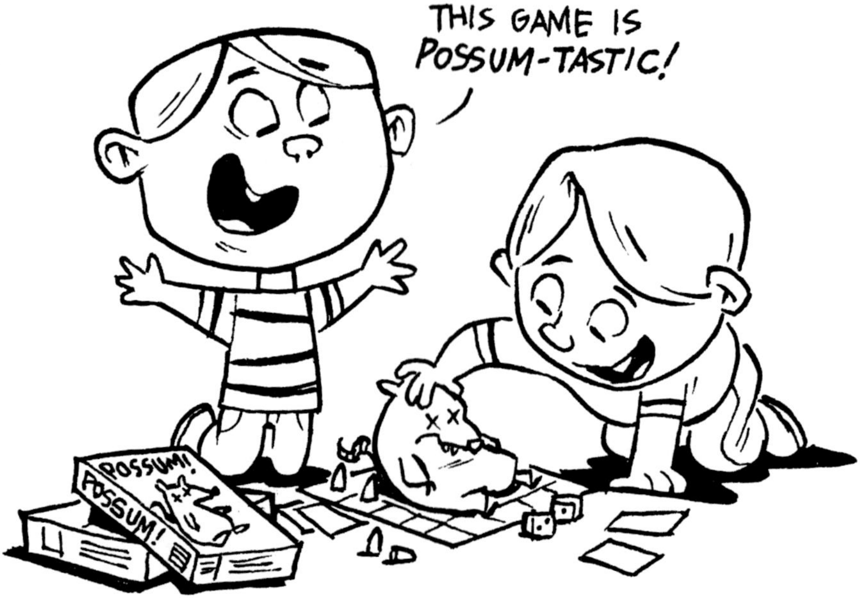
THIS GAME IS POSSUM-TASTIC!
POSSUM!
POSSUM!

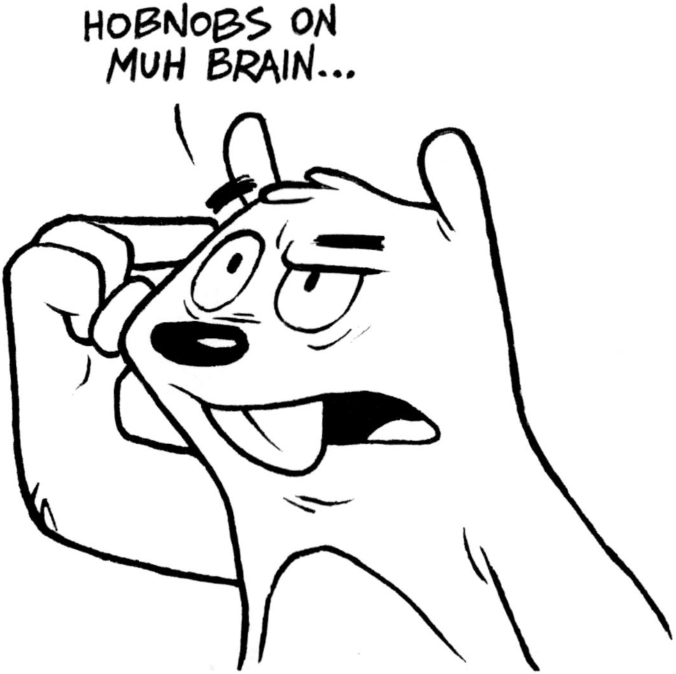
HOBNOBS ON MUH BRAIN...

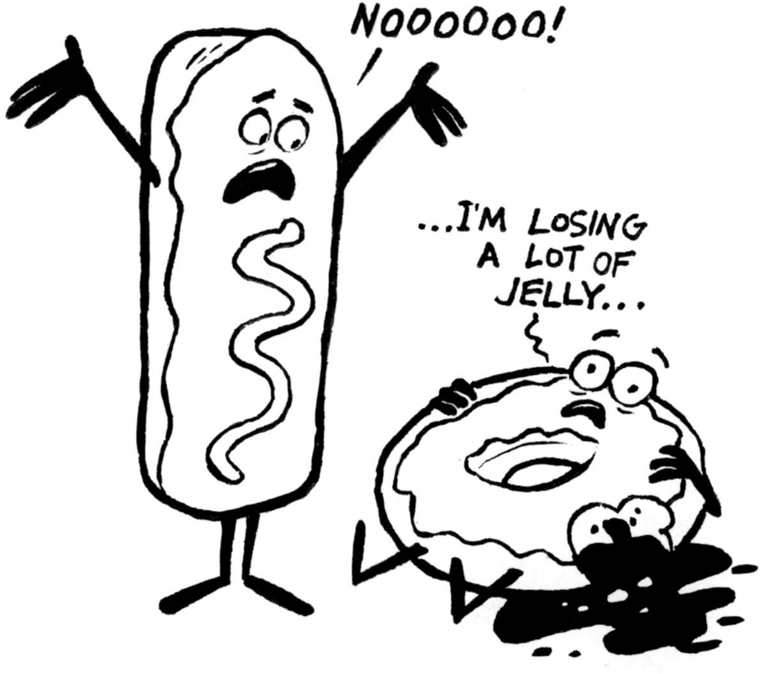
NOOOOOO!
...I'M LOSING A LOT OF JELLY...

swords.

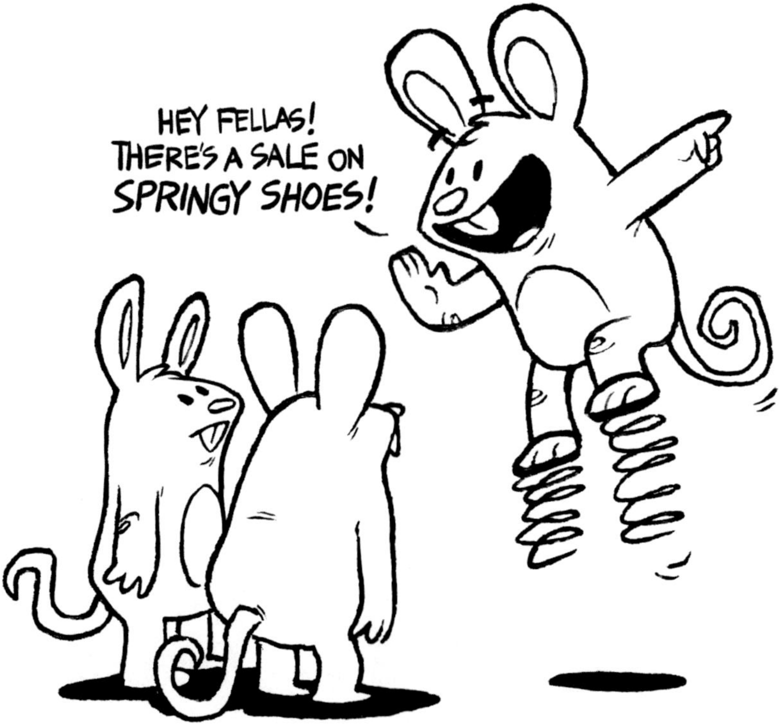
HEY FELLAS! THERE'S A SALE ON SPRINGY SHOES!

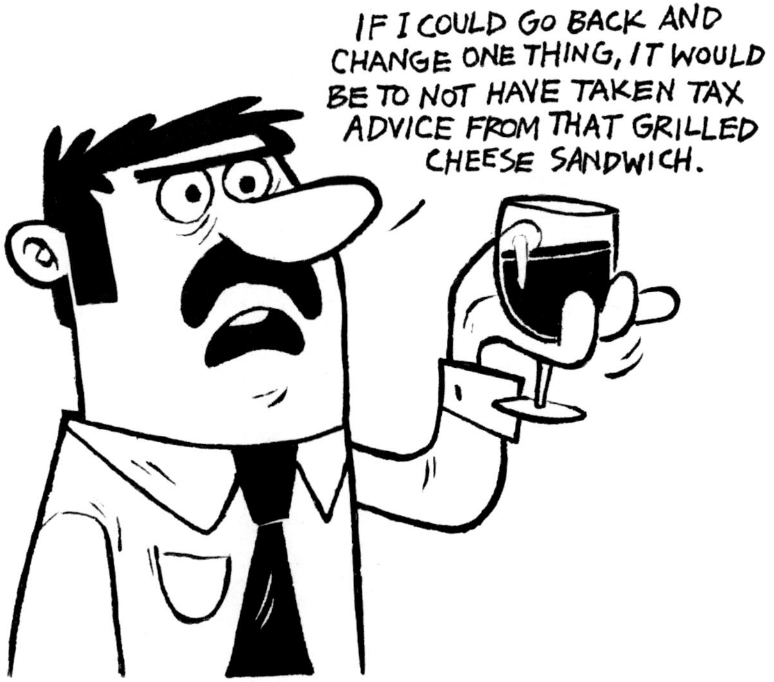
IF I COULD GO BACK AND CHANGE ONE THING, IT WOULD BE TO NOT HAVE TAKEN TAX ADVICE FROM THAT GRILLED CHEESE SANDWICH.

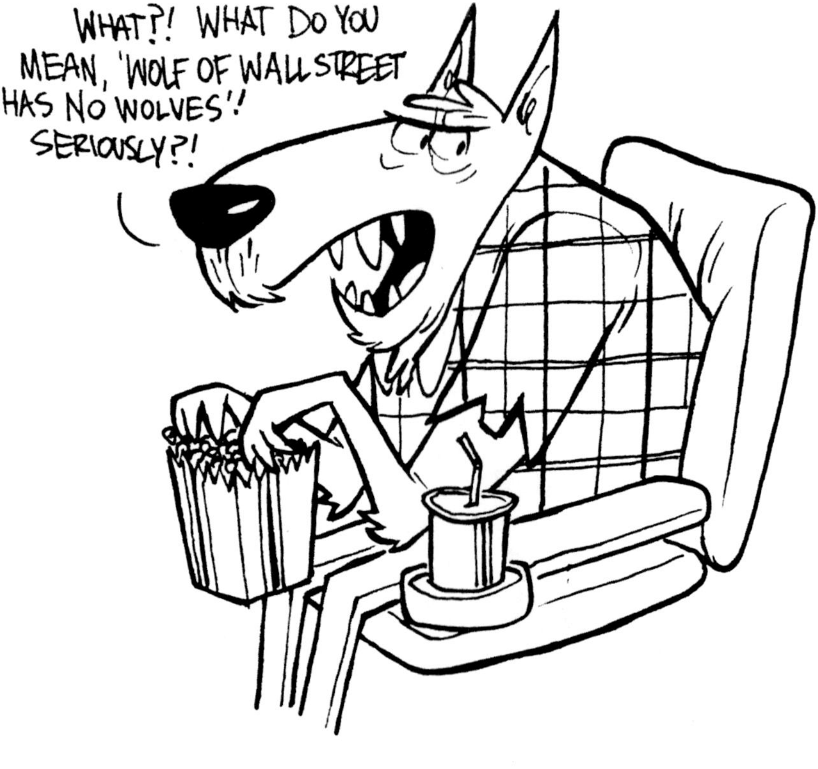
WHAT?! WHAT DO YOU MEAN, 'WOLF OF WALL STREET HAS NO WOLVES'! SERIOUSLY?!

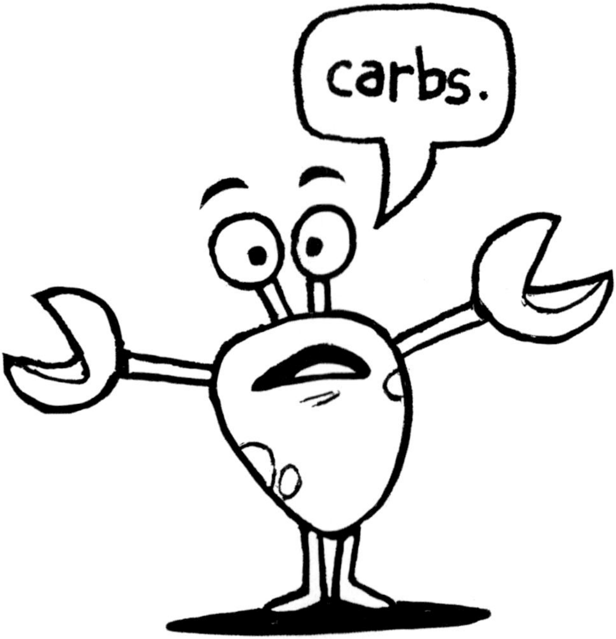
carbs.

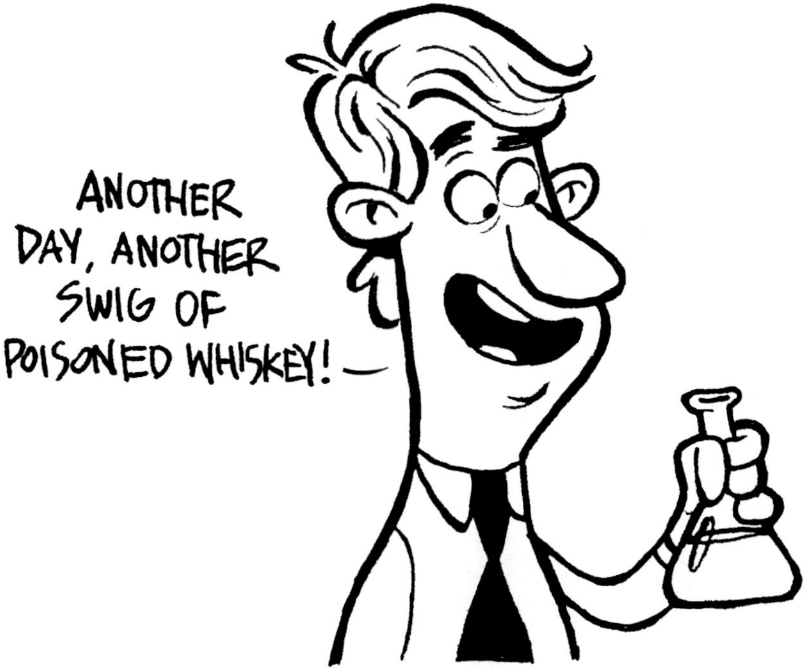
ANOTHER DAY, ANOTHER SWIG OF POISONED WHISKEY!

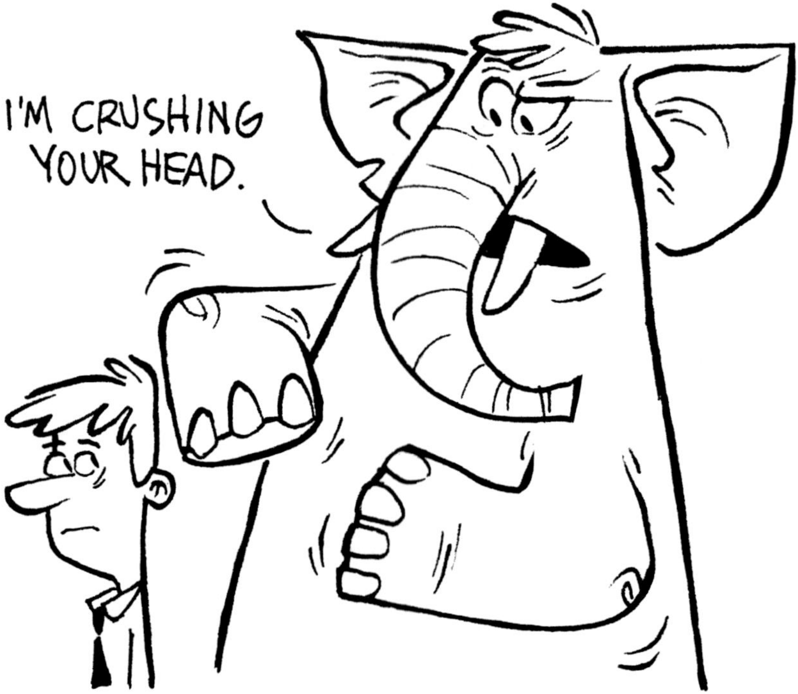
I'M CRUSHING YOUR HEAD.

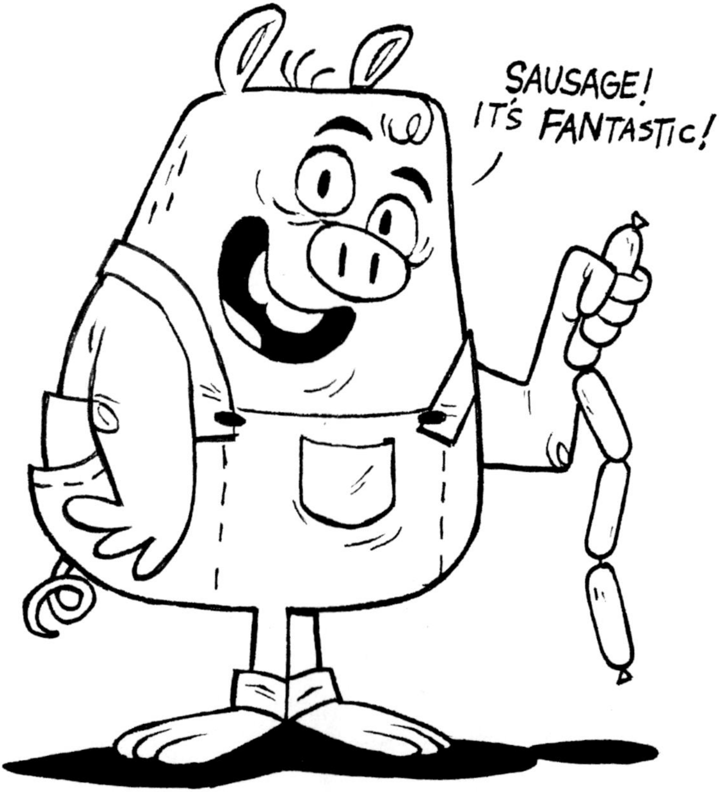
SAUSAGE!
IT'S FANTASTIC!

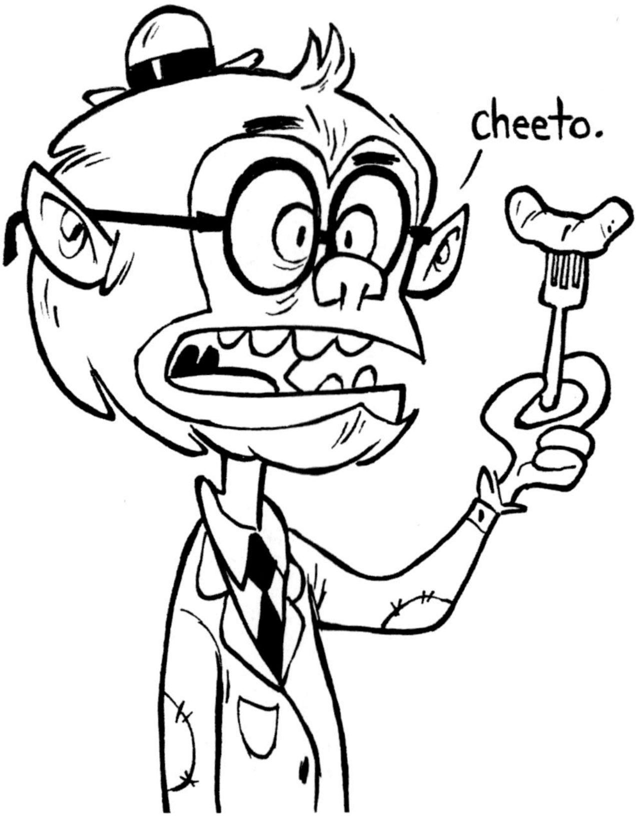
cheeto.

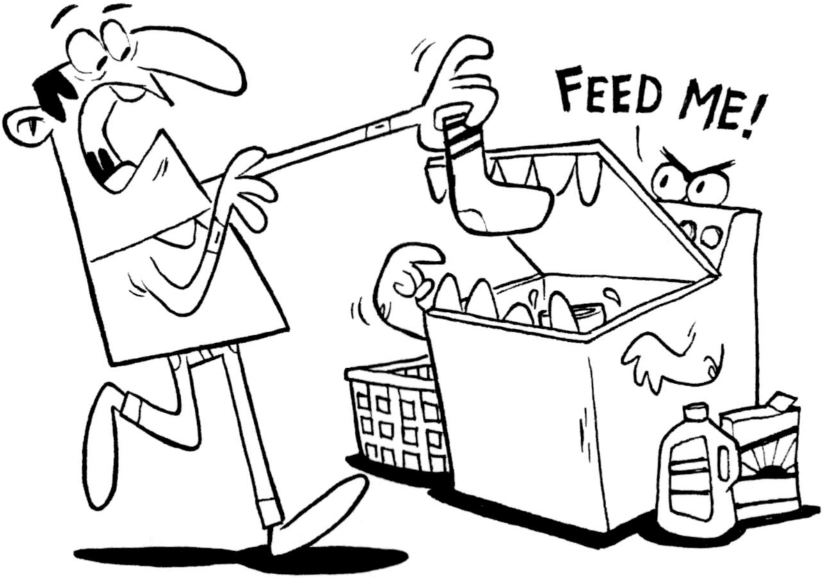
FEED ME!

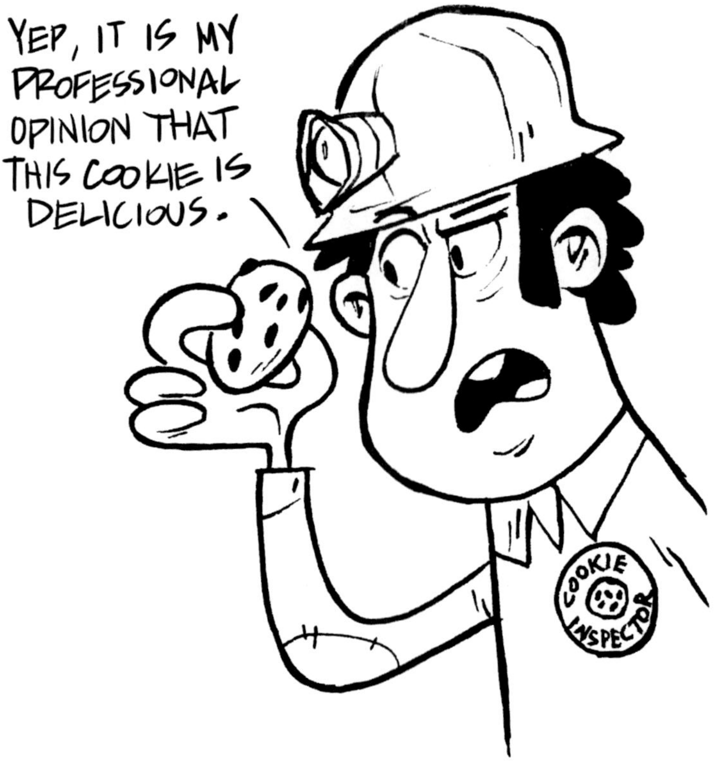
YEP, IT IS MY PROFESSIONAL OPINION THAT THIS COOKIE IS DELICIOUS.
COOKIE INSPECTOR

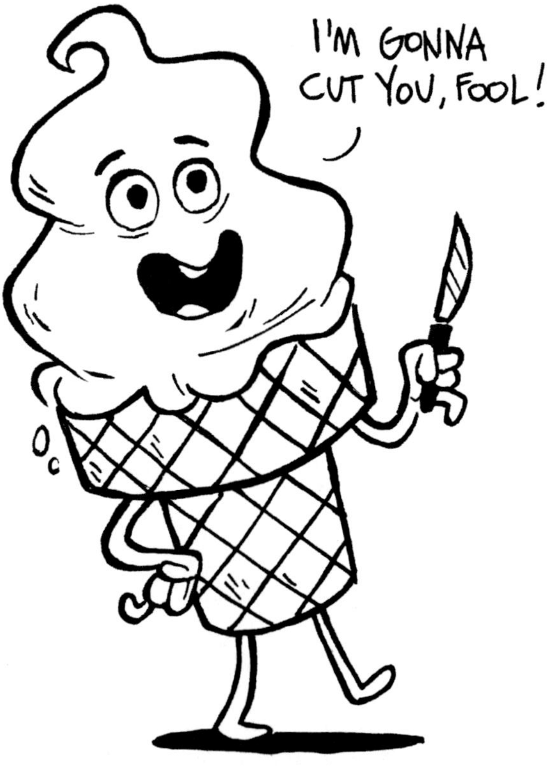
I'M GONNA
CUT YOU, FOOL!

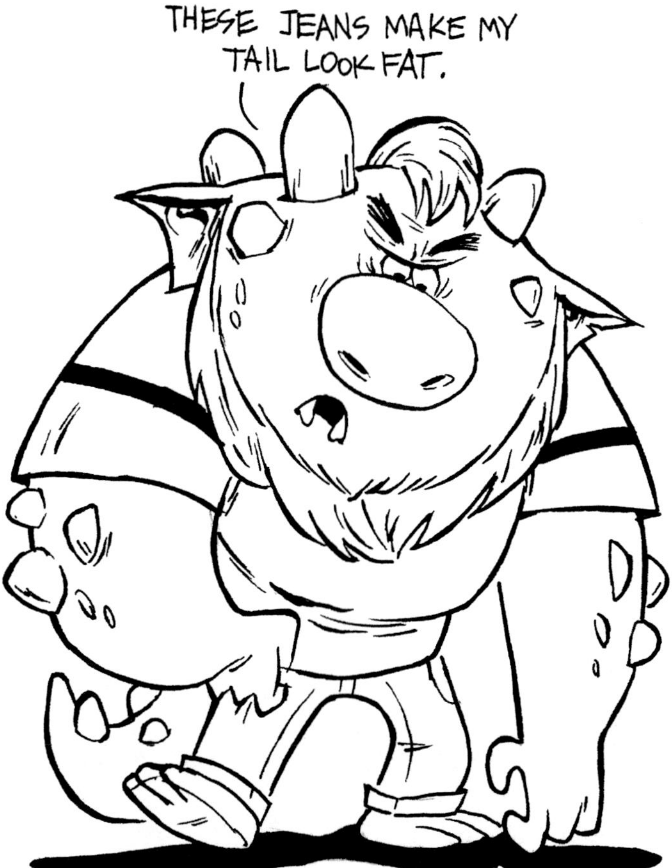
THESE JEANS MAKE MY TAIL LOOK FAT.